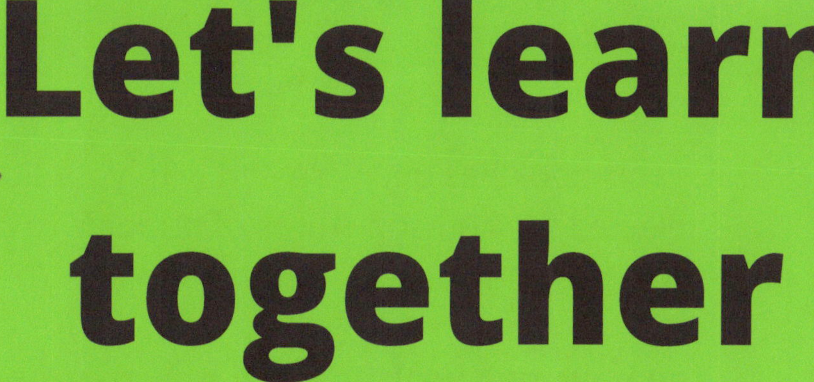

Let's learn together

Apprenons ensemble

This book has been created with your little one in mind.
We selected the cutest pictures of puppies to maintain the attention
of your cutie pie while stimulating her/his desire to learn.

**You have two ways to learn how to pronounce the words:
the phonetics and an audio track.**

About the phonetics: if you are not familiar with phonetics, quick research on
the internet about International Phonetics and you will learn all about it.

About the audio tracks: Juliette, my daughter, and I recorded the voices
in the QR codes, in English and French. Just scan the corresponding QR code
and voilà!

For the best experience, please download a QR Code Reader on your phone
(many are free!). You can also use the camera app
on most of the recent mobile phones.

We hope your family will enjoy reading this book as much as
we had fun creating it.

Thank you for choosing us!

Ce livre a été crée en pensant à votre petit trésor.
Nous avons sélectionné les plus adorables photos de chiots afin de
captiver l'attention de votre puce tout en stimulant son désir d'apprendre.

**Deux choix s'offrent à vous pour apprendre
la prononciation des mots dans chacune des langues:
la phonétique ou la piste audio du code QR.**

Phonétique: si vous n'êtes pas familier avec ce language, une simple
recherche sur internet vous apprendra les bases.

Piste audio: Juliette, ma fille, et moi avons enregistré les voix des codes QR.
Il vous suffit de lire le code QR correspondant à la langue de votre choix,
et voilà!

Pour une expérience optimale, veuillez télécharger un lecteur de code QR
sur votre téléphone mobile (plusieurs sont gratuits). L'application caméra
de la plupart des téléphones cellulaires récents peut aussi lire les codes.

Nous espérons que votre famille aura autant de plaisir à lire ce livre que
nous en avons eu à le créer.

Merci de nous avoir choisi!

apple

/ˈæpəl/

Français: pomme

/pɔm/

bathtub

/ˈbæθtəb/

Français: baignoire

/bɛ.ɲwaʁ/

clown

/klaʊn/

Français: clown

/klun/

deer

/dɪr/

Français: chevreuil

/ʃə.vʁœj/

egg

/ɛg/

Français: oeuf

/œf/

flower

/ˈflaʊər/

Français: fleur

/flœʁ/

gift

/gɪft/

Français: cadeau

/ka.do/

horse

/hɔrs/

Français: cheval

/ʃɛˈval/

ice cream

/aɪs krim/

Français: crème glacée

/kʀɛm gla.se/

jar

/d͡ʒar/

Français: pot

/po/

ATTENTION
Chien craquant

kitten

/ˈkɪtən/

Français: chaton

/ʃa.tɔ̃/

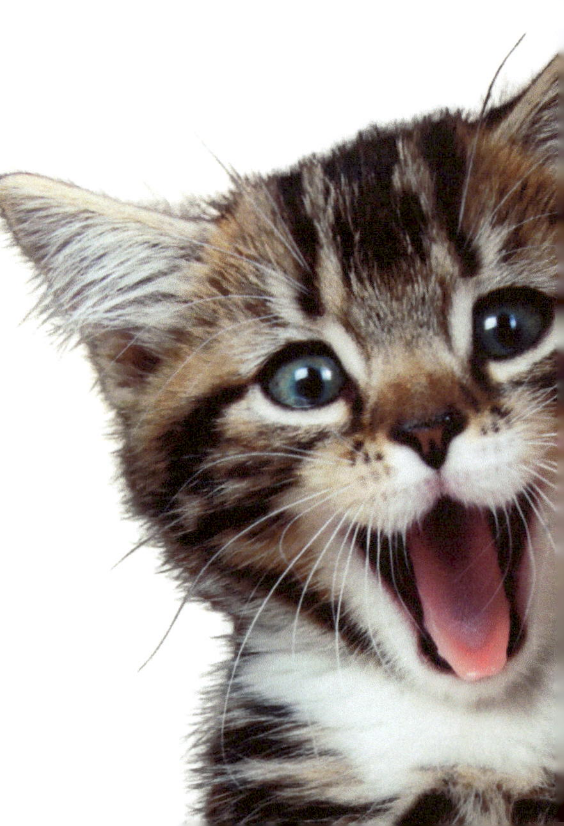

lawn
/lɔn/

Français: pelouse
/pə.luz/

mask

/mæsk/

Français: masque

/mask/

newspaper
/ˈnuzˌpeɪpər/

Français: journal
/ʒuʁ.nal/

DAILY DOG
MAY 23rd 1971
CHICO -A STAR IS BORN!
READING THE NEWS
TODAY
THE ARTICLE OF THE DAY
WINNING DOG
PLACES TO BE
HOW TO GET FAMOUS
MUNICH
NICE PLACES IN NEW YORK

ocean

/ˈoʊʃən/

Français: océan

/ɔ.se.ã/

paint

/peɪnt/

Français: peinture

/pɛ̃.tyʁ/

queen

/kwin/

Français: reine

/ʁɛn/

rose
/roʊz/

Français: rose
/ʀoz/

snow
/snoʊ/

Français: neige
/nɛʒ/

toothpaste

/ˈtuθˌpeɪst/

Français: dentifrice

/dɑ̃.ti.fʁis/

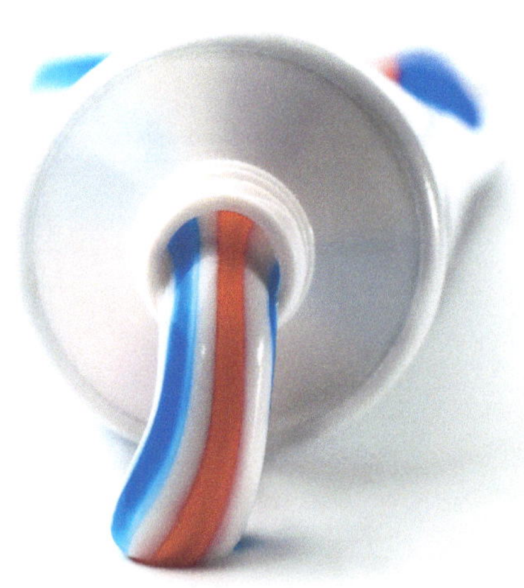

ukulele

/ˌjukəˈleɪli/

Français: ukulele

/juː.kə.ˈleɪ.li/

veggies

/ˈvɛdʒiz/

Français: légumes

/le.gym/

watermelon
/ˈwɔtərˌmɛlən/

Français: melon d'eau
/mə.lɔ̃ d‿o/

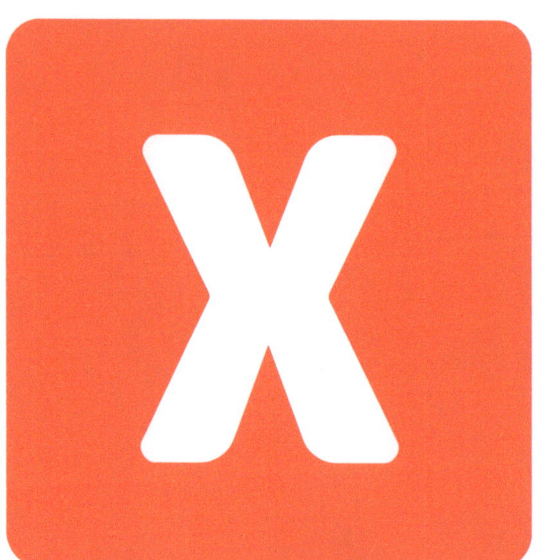

X-ray
/ˈɛksˌreɪ/

Français: rayon X
/ʁɛ.jɔ̃ iks/

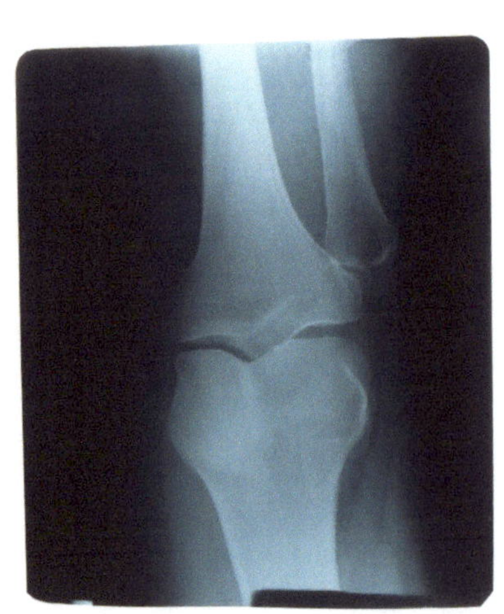

yawn

/jɔn/

Français: bâiller

/bɑ.je/

Z
Z
Z
Z
Z

zebra
/ˈzibrə/

Français: zèbre

/zɛbʁ/

**Original idea and creation/
Idée originale et création:**
Guylaine Doré

**English Narration/
Narration anglaise:**
Juliette Brosseau

**French Narration/
Narration française:**
Guylaine Doré

www.ingramcontent.com/pod-product-compliance
Lightning Source LLC
Chambersburg PA
CBHW042045110726
48006CB00002B/298